Disney · PIXAR
Cars

BIG BOOK OF
THINGS TO
MAKE
AND DO

PaRragon

Bath • New York • Singapore • Hong Kong • Cologne • Delhi
Melbourne • Amsterdam • Johannesburg • Auckland • Shenzhen

First published by Parragon in 2011

Parragon
Queen Street House
4 Queen Street
Bath BA1 1HE, UK

ISBN 978-1-4454-2523-8

Printed in China

CONTENTS

TIPS FOR SUCCESS

Remember, everything in this book should be made with the supervision and help of a grown up! A step labelled with "Kids" means that a child can do this step on their own. Some items will need to be purchased from a supermarket or a craft/hobby store.

1 Prepare your space

Cover your workspace with newspaper or a plastic or paper tablecloth. Make sure you and your children are wearing clothes (including shoes!) that you don't mind becoming spattered with food, paint, or glue. But relax! You'll never completely avoid mess; in fact, it's part of the fun!

2 Wash your hands

Wash your hands (and your child's hands) before starting a new project, and clean up as you go along. Clean hands make for clean crafts! Remember to wash hands afterwards too, using soap and warm water to get off any of the remaining materials.

3 Follow steps carefully

Follow each step carefully, and in the sequence in which it appears. We've tested all the projects; we know they work, and we want them to work for you, too.

4 Measure precisely

If a project gives you measurements, use your ruler, measuring scales, or measuring spoons to make sure you measure as accurately as you can. Sometimes, the success of the project may depend on it.

5 Be patient

You may need to wait while something bakes or leave paint, glue or clay to dry, sometimes for a few hours or even overnight. Be patient! Plan another activity while you wait, but it's important not to rush something as it may affect the outcome!

6 Clean up

When you've finished your project, clean up any mess. Store all the materials together so that they are ready for the next time you want to make and do. Remember it's a team effort!

READY, STEADY, GO! FRAME

Lightning knows all about photo finishes. Make this frame to capture all the racing action at a party or with your friends!

1

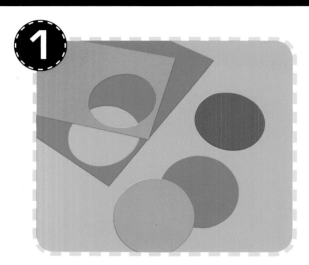

Draw three circles (about 5 inches (12cm) in diameter) onto card. One red, one amber and one green. Cut them out.

YOU WILL NEED

CARD

COLOURED PAPER

SCISSORS

GLUE

TAPE

CUPS/LIDS – SOMETHING TO DRAW AROUND

FOIL

RIBBON

Kids 2

Glue the three circles on a piece of black card. Leave to dry.

Kids 3

Glue the traffic lights onto some card which you have covered with foil. Tape a piece of ribbon to the back.

4

Cut out three photos into circles and stick them onto the traffic lights.

CHEQUERED RACE FLAG

Boost is always fast off the mark during a drifting race. Make this flag to host your own race at a party or just for fun!

YOU WILL NEED

THICK PAPER 28 X 40 INCHES (70CM X 100CM)

A PENCIL

A RULER

BLACK PAINT

SPONGE

A THIN STICK

TAPE

Kids 1

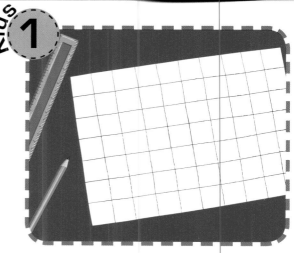

Divide a piece of white paper into squares with a pencil and ruler so you have a grid. Keep the pencil lines light – don't press too hard.

2

Cut a sponge to the same size as the squares. Dip the sponge into a saucer of black paint and practise printing squares onto some newspaper (or scrap paper).

Kids 3

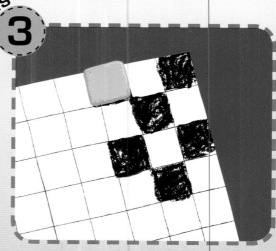

Print alternate black squares on the flag. Dip the sponge into paint for each new square. Dry.

Kids
4

BOOST'S GAME TIP: YOU NEED AT LEAST THREE PLAYERS TO HAVE A RACE. THE RACE OFFICIAL AND TWO COMPETITORS!

Wrap the end of the flag around a stick. Tape along the edge. Let's get waving your race flag!

RACING WHEELS

Guido and Luigi are tyre experts, and they know some good tyres when they see them...Like these!

YOU WILL NEED

PAPER

PENCIL

A ROLLING PIN

A COOKIE CUTTER

PENCIL OR COCKTAIL STICK - FOR MAKING HOLES

A BAKING TRAY

PAINTS

A KEY CHAIN

SALT DOUGH RECIPE:

2 CUPS (200G) PLAIN FLOUR

1 CUP (200G) OF SALT

1 CUP (200ML) OF WATER

1 TABLESPOON OF COOKING OIL

1

Mix up 2 cups (200g) of plain flour and 1 cup (200g) of salt in a mixing bowl. Add 1 cup (200ml) of water, and 1 tablespoon of oil to make a dough.

Kids **2**

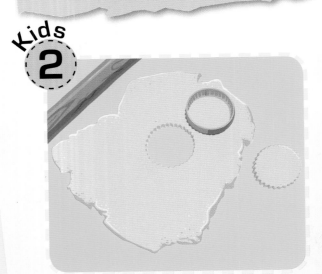

Knead the dough into a ball on a floured worksurface. Roll it out to 1¼ inches (1cm) thick. Cut out the wheel shapes using a cookie cutter.

3

Paint the circles black. When they dry you can highlight the pattern around the edge in a lighter colour. Keep paint fairly dry to do this.

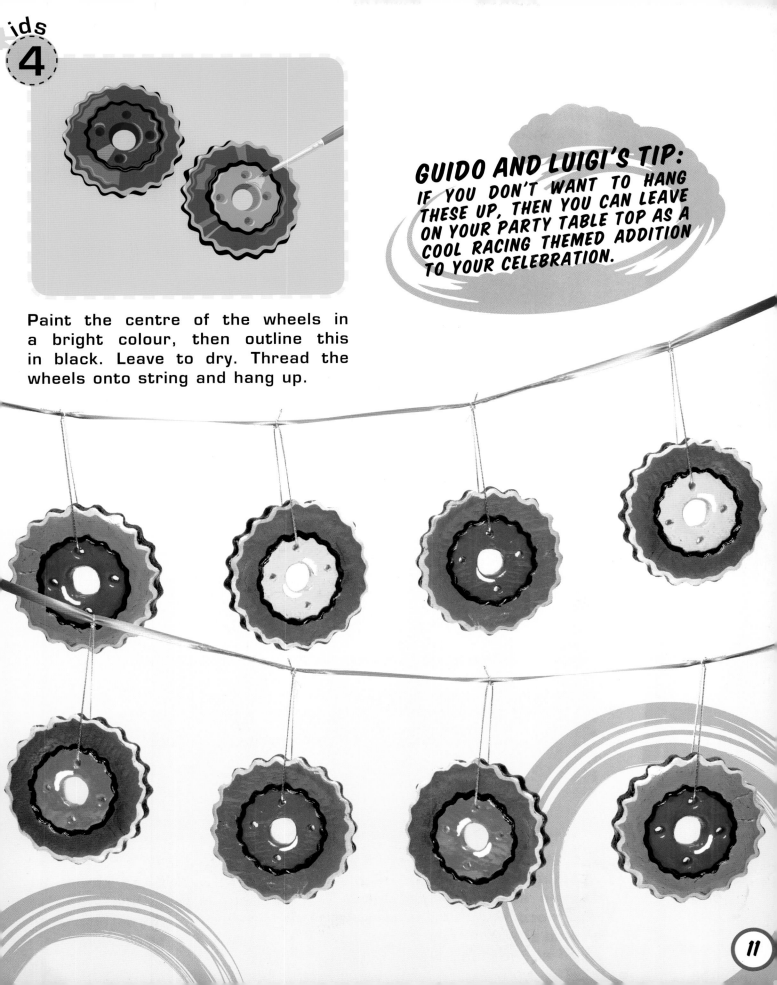

GUIDO AND LUIGI'S TIP: IF YOU DON'T WANT TO HANG THESE UP, THEN YOU CAN LEAVE ON YOUR PARTY TABLE TOP AS A COOL RACING THEMED ADDITION TO YOUR CELEBRATION.

Paint the centre of the wheels in a bright colour, then outline this in black. Leave to dry. Thread the wheels onto string and hang up.

PARTY CARS

Mater is a cheery character and full of surprises. Give these party cars to all your friends and family, they hold some unexpected treats and fun!

YOU WILL NEED

- CARDBOARD TUBES
- SCISSORS
- PAINT
- BLACK, RED, AND YELLOW CARD
- PAPER FASTENERS
- GLUE
- PARTY GIFTS – CANDY, BADGES, BALLOONS, ETC

1

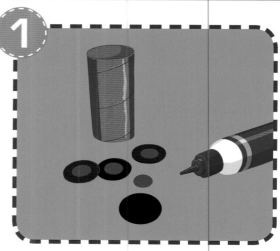

Paint a cardboard tube and allow it to dry. Cut out four wheels from black card, then glue smaller red circles to the middle of each wheel. Cut out a steering wheel.

2

Cut along the tube and make a rectangular hole in the middle. Glue a steering wheel inside. Add decoration either in paint or add shapes made from card, such as lightning bolts.

3

Make four holes in the tube where you want the wheels to go. Attach the wheels to the tube using paper fasteners.

4

Wrap a few small gifts/sweets into a piece of tissue paper. Twist the ends so the gifts won't fall out, then push inside the tube.

MATER'S TOP TIP:
YOU COULD WRITE YOUR FRIENDS' NAMES ON THEIR CARS FOR A SUPER SPECIAL FINISHING TOUCH!

FLO'S BURGERS

Flo knows how to cook up a storm in her café. Here's a special recipe that she has cooked up just for you and your party, come rain or shine!

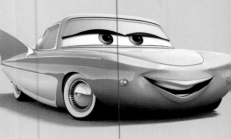

YOU WILL NEED

TO MAKE 4 BURGERS:

VEGETABLE OIL

1 SMALL ONION, CHOPPED

1 TEASPOON CHOPPED PARSLEY (OR HERB OF CHOICE)

½ CUP (70G) BREADCRUMBS

8-OUNCE (225G) CAN RED SALMON

OR TUNA PACKED WITH WATER

1 EGG

SALT AND PEPPER TO TASTE

FLOUR

LETTUCE, TOMATO SLICES, ONION RINGS, MAYONNAISE

4 WHOLEWHEAT BURGER BUNS

PAN

1

Heat two teaspoonfuls of oil in the pan; add the onion, herbs, and breadcrumbs and sauté gently for five minutes.

Kids 2

Pour the mixture into a bowl and let cool. Add the fish, egg, salt and pepper. Mix everything together with your hands.

Kids 3

Sprinkle some flour onto the work surface and shape the mixture into burgers.

4 Wash and dry the pan, add oil, and place over medium heat. Fry the burger for five minutes on each side.

Kids

5 Put each burger on a bun and garnish with lettuce, tomato slices, onion rings and mayonnaise.

FLO'S TIP:
SERVE THESE TASTY TREATS ON YOUR RACETRACK TABLETOP, WITH WHEEL DECORATIONS AND MINI CHEQUERED FLAGS!

STARS OF CARS COOKIES

Ramone loves stars, or flames, or lightning bolts. In fact anything that stands out! Make these quirky shaped cookies and wow your friends!

YOU WILL NEED

LARGE MIXING BOWL

SIEVE

2 ¼ CUPS (250G) ALL-PURPOSE FLOUR

PINCH OF SALT

1 TEASPOON BAKING POWDER

1 TABLESPOON BUTTER

¾ CUP (170G) LIGHT BROWN SUGAR

2 EGGS, BEATEN

2 OUNCES (55G) CORN SYRUP

3 OUNCES (85G) CHOCOLATE

ROLLING PIN

A COOKIE CUTTER

NONSTICK COOKING SPRAY

BAKING SHEET

1

Pre-heat the oven to 325°F (170°C, GM 3). Sift the flour, salt and baking powder into a large bowl.

Kids 2

With your fingers, rub the butter into the dry ingredients. Add the sugar. In a cup, stir together the eggs and the corn syrup.

Kids 3

With a wooden spoon, beat the ingredients until they are thoroughly combined. Break the chocolate into small chunks and add to the mixture.

4

5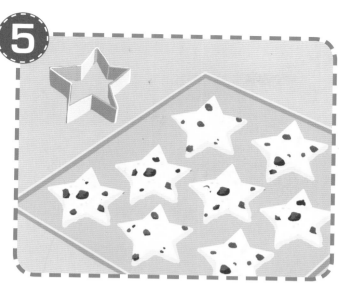

Place the dough on a board. Sprinkle it lightly with flour so it doesn't stick to the rolling pin. Roll out the dough until it's about ½-inch (1.25cm) thick. With a cookie cutter, cut out the cookies, like these star-shaped cookies.

Lightly grease a baking sheet with nonstick cooking spray or vegetable oil. Place the cookies about 2 inches (5cm) apart on the baking sheet. Bake for about 15 minutes, until golden.

RAMONE'S TOP TIP:
EXPERIMENT WITH DIFFERENT COOKIE SHAPES JUST LIKE I EXPERIMENT WITH MY PAINT DESIGNS!

LIGHTNING MCQUEEN

- **VEHICLE: ONE-OF-A-KIND RACING CAR**

- **COLOUR: RED**

- **PROS: ENOUGH MOTOR POWER AND DRIVE TO MATCH 10 RACING CARS**

- **PROFILE:**
  FOUR-TIME winner of the Piston Cup, **LIGHTNING** is a **WORLD FAMOUS** race car! He is always surrounded by his friends from Radiator Springs, including his best friend, **MATER**. When **LIGHTNING** enters the first ever World Grand Prix, he's up against some of the best race cars in the world!

KA-CHOWW!

"I am speed!" chanted Lightning McQueen as he focused on the dirt track stretched out in front of him. Standing by were Luigi and the Pit Crew. Lightning revved his engine – VAA-ROOOM – and took off! As he turned, he suddenly lost control and went off the track.

Watching in the wings was Doc. "I told ya to steer right to go left." he called out. Lightning wanted to call it a day and head back to town and get cleaned up. But Doc was determined to make Lightning practise the turn again. Doc gave Lightning a pep talk – no worrying about his silly paint job, no more whining and no more rest until he got the turn right!

Lightning tried the turn again and again. He became more determined than ever, and concentrating on Doc's advice, he roared down the dirt track ... As he neared the curve, he glided around the corner – and stayed on the track!

"Ka-choww!" hooted Lightning as he headed towards the finish line. Lightning then turned to Doc and challenged him to a spin around the track. Doc smiled and sped off. The race was on!

TURN THE PAGE

MINI RACERS

These cars have some real wind power behind them. Make them, then race them. You create the horsepower!

1

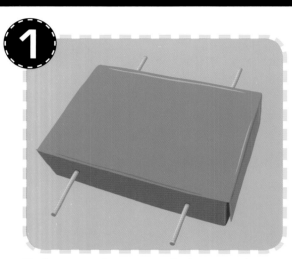

Paint a box and leave it to dry. Push two wooden skewers through the sides to make axles. Use a pencil to make a hole first. This makes it easier to push the skewers through the box.

Kids 2

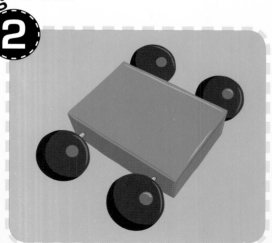

Push the polystyrene balls onto the skewers with a blob of glue on the end.

YOU WILL NEED

2 SMALL BOXES

POLYSTYRENE BALLS

2 WOODEN SKEWERS

GLUE

PAINT

BRUSH

COLOURED CARD

WOBBLY EYES

2 PIECES OF THICK CARD FOR PROPELLING THE CARS.

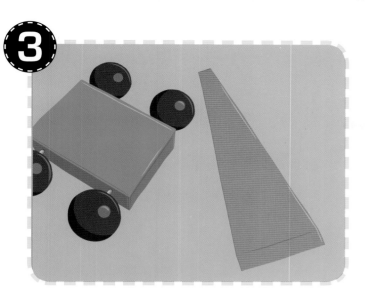

Cut a triangular piece of card. It needs to be about one and a half times the length of your car and the same width.

Stick the triangle onto the cars so it makes a curved shape. Add eyes. Make another car using different colours so you can have a race.

LIGHTNING'S RACING TIP:
PLACE THE CARS ON A SMOOTH FLOOR. WAVE A PIECE OF CARD UP AND DOWN JUST BEHIND THE CARS TO CREATE A DRAUGHT WHICH WILL PROPEL THEM ALONG. WHOEVER DOES THIS THE FASTEST WILL WIN.

RACETRACK TABLETOP MANIA

Doc has raced on some very unique racetracks in his time. Create your own one-of-a-kind track below!

YOU WILL NEED

LARGE SHEETS OF PAPER

TAPE

PENS, PENCILS, CRAYONS

DOC'S TOP TIP:
THIS IS A FUN WAY TO ADD SOME EXTRA RACING FUN TO A PARTY. MAKE THE TRACK THEN USE IT AS A TABLECLOTH!

1

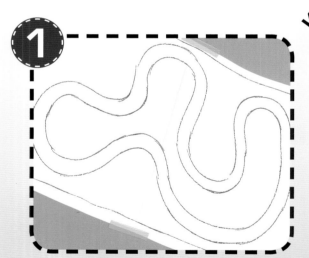

Tape down a large sheet of paper to cover a table. It will depend on the size of paper and size of table. Lightly outline a racetrack and a border in pencil.

Kids **2**

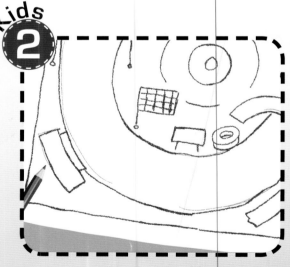

Sit your friends around the table next to different areas on the race track. Go over the pencil lines with crayons or felt pen then add details like flags and banners.

Colour in the different areas of the racetrack. Big areas can be filled in quickly by rubbing big crayons on their side.

Add everyone's names around the edge of the track. Then admire your handy work like true racing pros.

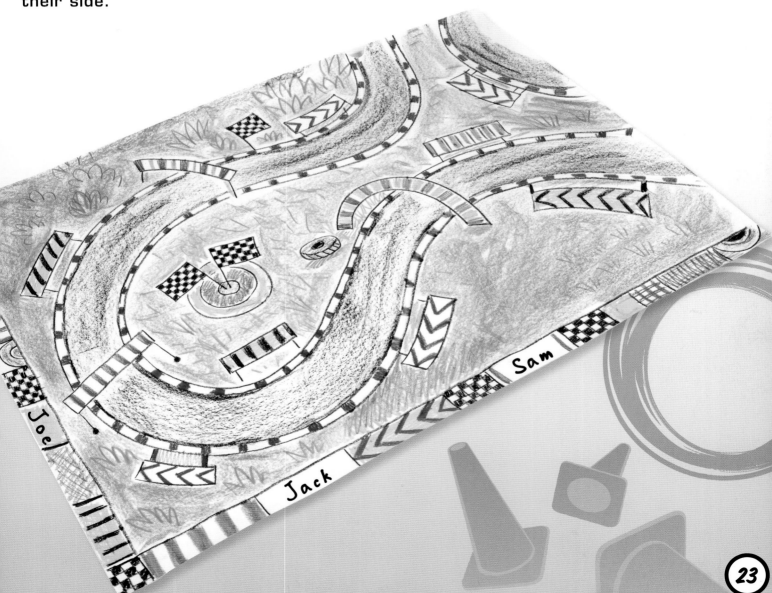

TARGET GAME

Boost is always on target when he drifts to the max on sharp bends. Have you got the same skills? Let's find out!

YOU WILL NEED

- A SHOE BOX WITH A LIFT UP LID
- TAPE
- PAINT
- BRUSH
- CRAFT FOAM
- GLUE AND SCISSORS
- A SMALL RUBBER BALL

Kids 1

Lift up the lid of the box. Tape it into an upright position.

Kids 2

Paint the inside of the lid blue. Leave to dry then paint desert colours on the inside and sides of the box. Leave to dry.

3

Cut out simple cactus and palm tree shapes from craft foam. Print patterns using the end of a straw and strips of foam dipped in paint.

BOOST'S GAME TIPS:
TAKE IT IN TURNS TO BOUNCE THE
BALL AIMING FOR THE BOX! THE
WINNER IS THE FIRST TO GET THE
BALL IN THE BOX FIVE TIMES.

When the paint has dried, glue the
foam cactus and palm tree shapes
together then stick them onto to the
box.

TYRE THROWING

This tyre-tastic game will have you in a spin!

YOU WILL NEED

- SCISSORS
- A CARDBOARD TUBE
- THICK PIECE OF CARD – CUT FROM A BOX
- GLUE
- PAPER PLATES – 3 FOR EACH TYRE
- BLACK PAINT
- BRUSH

1

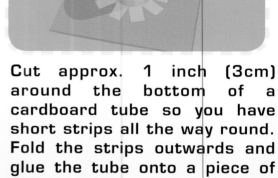

Cut approx. 1 inch (3cm) around the bottom of a cardboard tube so you have short strips all the way round. Fold the strips outwards and glue the tube onto a piece of thick card.

2

Cut a circle out from the middles of three paper plates. Glue them together in a stack.

Kids 3

Paint the circles black. When they dry you can highlight the pattern around the edge in a lighter colour.

GUIDO AND LUIGI'S GAME TIPS:

FOR THIS GAME YOU NEED TWO PLAYERS. TAKE IT IN TURNS TO THROW THE TYRES. THE FIRST PERSON TO GET FIVE ON THE STAND IS A TOP TYRE THROWER!

Paint the tube. Leave to dry. You are now all set to start throwing some tyres around!

RACE AND PLAY MAT

Mater loves his home town of Radiator Springs. When you've made this play mat you'll love it just as much as him!

YOU WILL NEED

- A SINGLE SHEET
- ACRYLIC PAINTS
- CARD
- MASKING TAPE
- PENCIL
- PAINTS AND BRUSHES
- SCISSORS
- SPONGES
- FABRIC PENS / FELT PENS

1

Spread the sheet out over some newspaper with a big piece of card underneath (cut from a box). Draw the outline of the roads in pencil then fill in with paint. Dry.

Kids

2

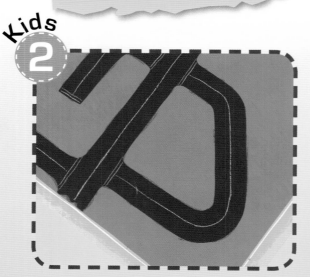

Paint yellow lines onto the roads. Leave to dry thoroughly. It will dry more quickly if you hang it outside on a clear day, on a washing line.

3

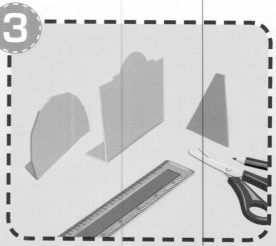

Cut simple card shapes for buildings, trees and rocky shapes. Stick card strips to the back so they stand up.

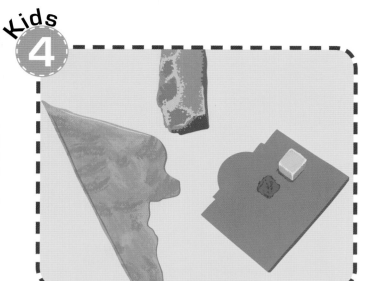

Use small pieces of sponge for printing the windows onto the buildings. Sponge texture onto the rocks and trees. Set your play mat out and get ready for a *Cars* adventure!

MATER'S TOP TIP:
YOUR PLAY MAT IS YOUR OWN NEW RACING WORLD, SO YOU CAN MAKE IT HOW YOU WANT IT! YOU'RE KING OF THE ROAD!

CAR-RAZY SKITTLES

Play skittles outdoors or, if it's raining, indoors. Roll a ball at the skittles and try to knock as many over as you can.

YOU WILL NEED

6 IDENTICAL CLEAR PLASTIC DRINKS BOTTLES WITH LIDS

READY-MIXED PAINTS: RED, YELLOW, GREEN

DISH WASHING LIQUID

OLD JUG

SELF-ADHESIVE STAR STICKERS

FUNNEL

SAND

BALL

1

In an old jug, mix the green paint with water until it looks like soup. Add a small squirt of dish washing liquid.

Kids

2

Pour some paint mixture into a bottle and put the top on. Shake the bottle to spread the paint all over the inside of the bottle. Add more paint if you need to.

3

Remove the top, pour out any remaining paint and let the bottle dry. Repeat for the other bottles, making three red, two green and one yellow skittles.

Put the funnel in the neck of the bottle and pour in sand until half full. This makes the skittles harder to knock over. Repeat for each of the bottles.

Put the tops back tightly on the bottles. Decorate the skittles with self-adhesive stickers.

SALLY'S TIP:
PAINTING THE SKITTLES FROM THE INSIDE OF THE BOTTLE MEANS THE PAINT WON'T CHIP WHEN YOU PLAY WITH THEM.

CHUTE SHOWDOWN

This game is not for the faint hearted. It's fast, furious and seriously fun!

YOU WILL NEED

- A LONG CARDBOARD TUBE
- A LARGE CARDBOARD BOX
- CARD
- SMALL CARDBOARD TUBE
- PAINTS
- BRUSH
- GLUE AND SCISSORS

1

Cut a long cardboard tube in half lengthways! Tape a small card flap to the end of each tube.

Kids 2

Make two small slots in the top of each box for the card flaps to fit into. This will hold the tubes securely at an angle and stop them from slipping off the box.

3

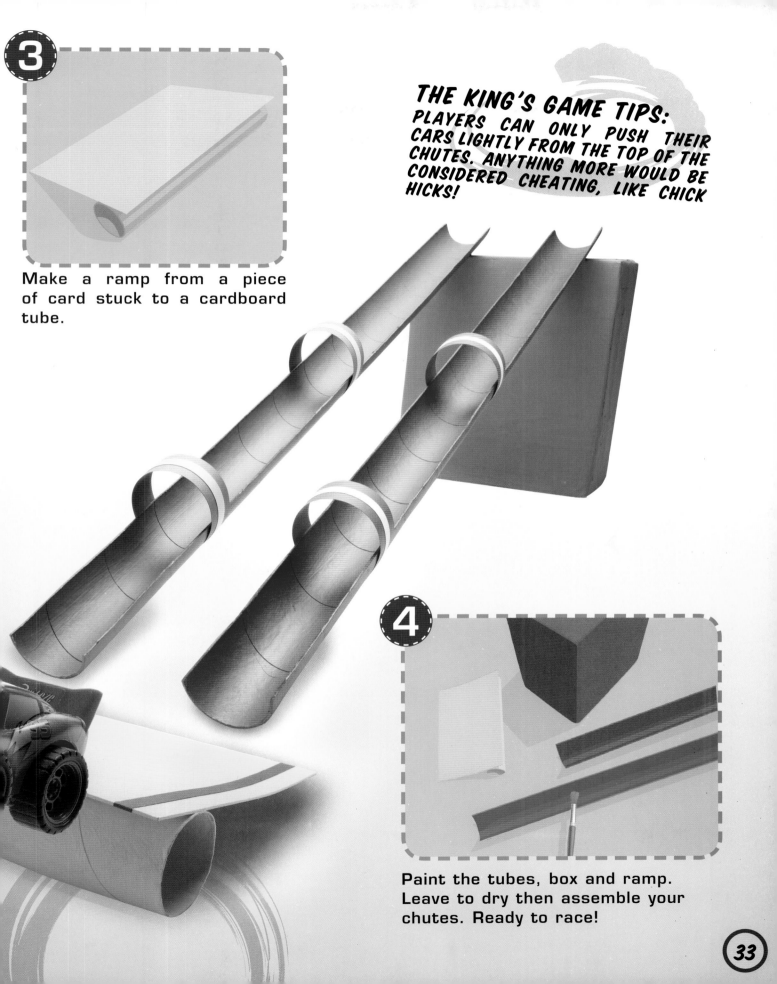

Make a ramp from a piece of card stuck to a cardboard tube.

THE KING'S GAME TIPS: PLAYERS CAN ONLY PUSH THEIR CARS LIGHTLY FROM THE TOP OF THE CHUTES. ANYTHING MORE WOULD BE CONSIDERED CHEATING, LIKE CHICK HICKS!

4

Paint the tubes, box and ramp. Leave to dry then assemble your chutes. Ready to race!

RED

- **VEHICLE: MID-1960S CLOSED-CAP PUMPER FIRE ENGINE**

- **COLOUR: RED**

- **PROS: WELL-LIKED BY THE OTHER CARS AND FRIENDLY**

- **PROFILE:**
  He is **SHY** and **VERY SENSITIVE**. Red spends most of his time gardening and washing things, such as the statue of **STANLEY** next to his **FIRE STATION**.

RED'S TUNE-UP BLUES

One morning, Red thought it was the perfect day to plant a garden. As he started his engine, a funny 'Pop! Pop!' noise came out of his tailpipe. He hoped that whatever was wrong would go away, because he didn't want to go to Doc's clinic. He didn't like the idea of being poked and prodded. As he headed into town, he soon passed Lightning McQueen.

Lightning greeted his friend and then heard a 'Bang! Bang!' sound coming from Red's engine. Lightning was worried about Red and headed to Flo's V8 café where he met his friends, Sally, Mater, Luigi, Guido, Fillmore and Flo. They tried to convince Red to visit Doc. Ramone even offered a new coat of paint at his House of Body Art, but nothing would make Red go.

'Bang! Pop, pop!, Red's engine gurgled louder. Sally reassured Red that although going for a tune-up can be scary, whatever was wrong with his engine could be fixed. It was better to get it checked sooner, or it could turn into a bigger problem later. Red knew what Sally said was true.

Later that day, Red rolled out of the clinic and all his friends were waiting for him. Red revved his engine. VROOM! It sounded smooth as silk. It was great to be running on all cylinders again!

TURN THE PAGE

PLAY A SPLASHING GAME WITH BIG RED!

WATER PISTOL GAME

Big Red has put out many a fire with his water cannons, and this game is all about super soaking mayhem!

Kids

1

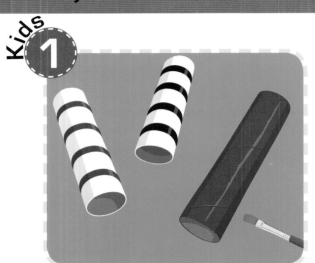

Paint some cardboard tubes in different colours. Leave to dry.

YOU WILL NEED

- CARDBOARD TUBES
- PAINT
- BRUSH
- COLOURED CARD
- WATER PISTOLS
- CLEAR STICKY FILM
- SCISSORS

2

Cut out some squares 8 x 8 inches (20 x 20cm) and circles 8 inches (20cm) in diameter from yellow card. Add simple cut out symbols.

3

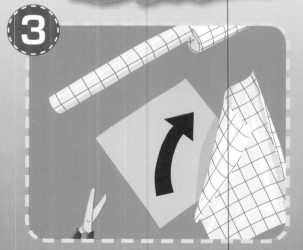

Cover each sign with clear sticky film to protect it from the super soaking water pistols.

BIG RED'S GAME TIPS:
SET THE SIGNS UP ON AN OUTDOOR TABLE OR WALL. HAVE A COMPETITION TO SEE WHO CAN KNOCK OVER THE MOST WITH A BIG WATER BLASTER!

Glue the signs onto the cardboard tubes. Stand back and start shooting the water!

ALL HOOKED UP

Mater's powerful hook can haul anything. Have a go at hooking these tools, in this fun game!

YOU WILL NEED

CRAFT FOAM

CARD

PENCIL

SCISSORS

GLUE

TAPE

PAPERCLIPS

2 PAINTED WOODEN STICKS / SKEWERS

THREAD OR WOOL

1

Draw some simple tool shapes onto card. Cut them out.

2

Draw around the tool shapes onto different coloured pieces of craft foam. Cut them out and stick together.

Kids

3

Glue a bent paperclip onto each foam tool. Leave to dry.

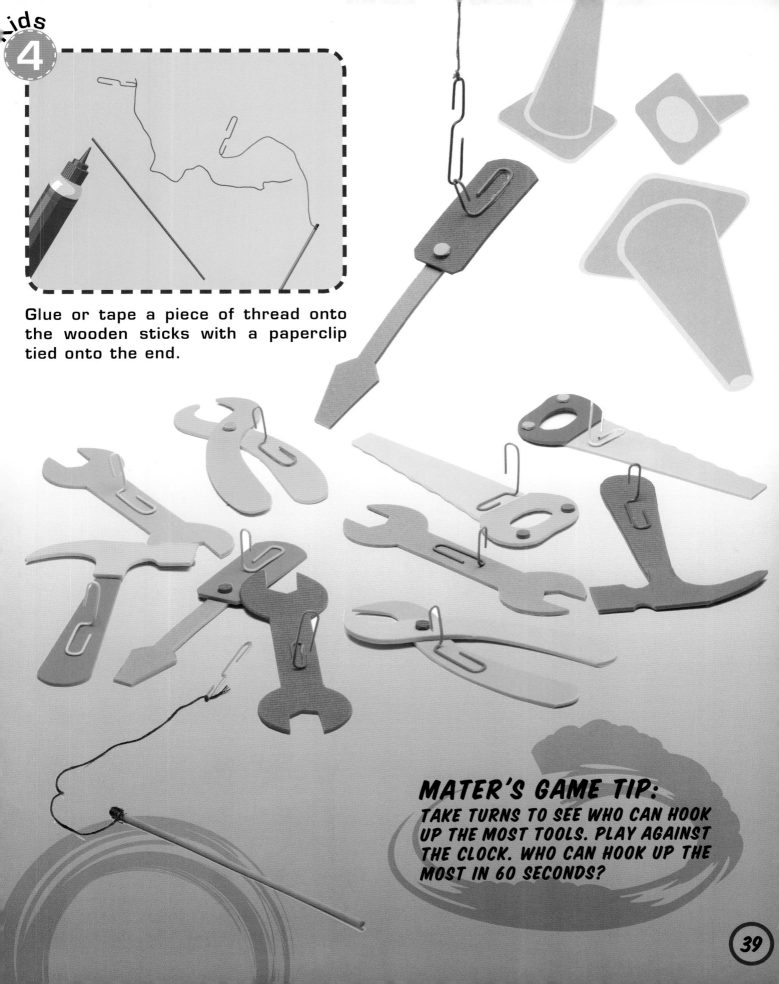

Glue or tape a piece of thread onto the wooden sticks with a paperclip tied onto the end.

MATER'S GAME TIP:
TAKE TURNS TO SEE WHO CAN HOOK UP THE MOST TOOLS. PLAY AGAINST THE CLOCK. WHO CAN HOOK UP THE MOST IN 60 SECONDS?

TABLETOP FOOTBALL

Sarge never gets puffed out. He's a top army car. Will you be able to win this game of fearsome staying power?

1

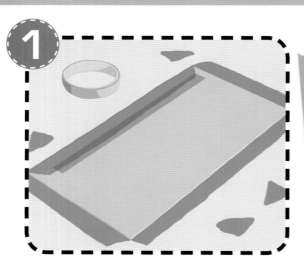

Cover the cardboard with the green felt, pull it tight, and tape it at the back.

YOU WILL NEED

- SHEET OF CARDBOARD, 20 X 28 INCHES (50 X 70CM)
- GREEN FELT
- STICKY TAPE
- WOOD GLUE
- WOOD BATONS: 2 X 28 INCHES (70CM), 2 X 20 INCHES (50CM)
- ACRYLIC PAINTS: YELLOW, WHITE
- SCISSORS
- SMALL CARDBOARD BOX
- RED PAPER
- 4 TOOTHPICKS
- DRINKING STRAW AND A PING-PONG BALL

Kids
2

Turn it over and draw field markings lightly in pencil. Paint over the lines in white.

Kids
3

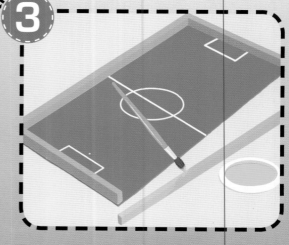

Paint the wood batons yellow and glue them together to make a fence around the field.

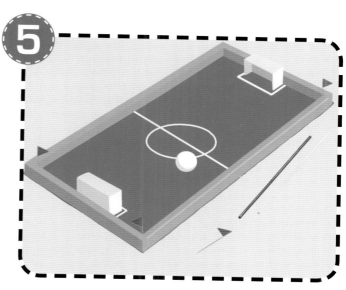

4 Cut a small cardboard box in half to make goals.

SARGE'S TOP TIP:
IF YOU'VE GOT PLENTY OF PUFF, TRY A GAME OF BLOW SOCCER. AND REMEMBER NO HANDS ALLOWED!

5 Put the goals inside the white boxes on the field. Cut out four small paper triangles and glue them to toothpicks to make corner flags.

NAUGHTS AND CROSSES MANIA

Tex is great at spotting the next racing talent! Will he spot you as the next O's and X's champion?

YOU WILL NEED

FOAM: 1 SHEET EACH IN BLACK, ORANGE, PURPLE, AND GREEN

SHEET OF THICK CARDBOARD 8 X 8 INCHES (50 X 50CM)

RULER

SCISSORS

WHITE GLUE AND BRUSH

PAPER AND PENCIL

1

Cut an 8 x 8 inch (50 x 50cm) square of black foam and glue it to the sheet of thick cardboard.

2

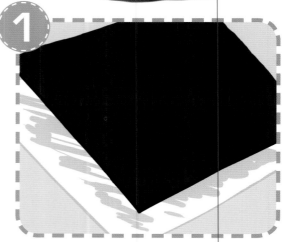

Use the ruler and pencil to draw four strips on the orange foam, 8 inches long and about ¼ inch (0.5cm) wide. Cut them out.

Kids 3

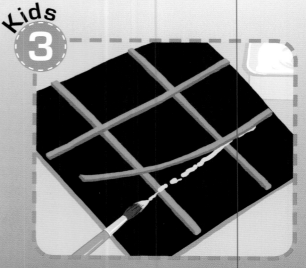

Glue the four strips of orange foam to the black foam in a crisscross shape. You can use the ruler to help you position them evenly.

4

Cut the green funky foam in half and glue the halves together to make a double-thick sheet. Repeat with the purple foam.

5

Draw a large "X" and an "O" onto the paper. Cut the shapes out and trace them onto the foam. Make five green "Xs" and five purple "Os". Cut out the shapes, and you're ready to play!

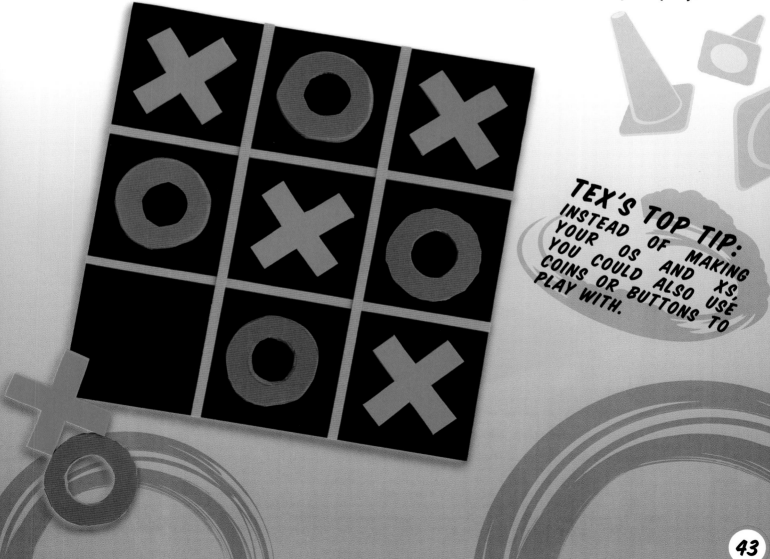

TEX'S TOP TIP:
INSTEAD OF MAKING YOUR OS AND XS, YOU COULD ALSO USE COINS OR BUTTONS TO PLAY WITH.

TRAVEL DRAUGHTS

Doc knows how to calculate a race and win it. Can you calculate how to win this brain powered game?

1

Cut around the bottom of the shoe box to make a tray about 2 inches (5cm) deep.

YOU WILL NEED

SHOE BOX

SCISSORS

ACRYLIC PAINTS: RED, WHITE, BLUE

PAINTBRUSH

WHITE GLUE AND BRUSH

RULER AND PENCIL

SHEETS OF PAPER: 1 WHITE,

1 BLUE

OVEN-BAKE CLAY: GREEN AND YELLOW

PLASTIC KNIFE

2

Paint the lid and the tray red all over. You might need to do several coats to cover all the lettering. Let dry.

3

Measure the width of the tray and cut your paper into a square the same size. Draw a grid on the paper of 8 x 8 squares.

4

Make a grid exactly the same size on the blue paper. Cut out the blue squares and stick them onto the white grid, so that alternate squares are blue.

5

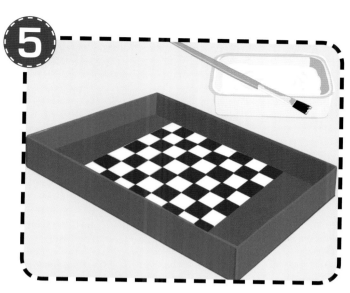

Spread white glue on the back of the paper and stick it down inside the box.

6

Roll each piece of clay into a sausage shape and use the plastic knife to slice each one into 12 counters. Bake them according to the manufacturer's instructions.

DOC'S TIP:
DON'T FORGET THIS IS A TRAVEL GAME! YOU CAN TAKE IT IN THE CAR, ON THE BUS, ON THE PLANE OR EVEN A BOAT!

MINI RACING FLAGS

Fillmore is a friendly car who loves to share. Make some yummy party food to share with your friends and rev it up with these cool mini racing flags!

YOU WILL NEED

PAPER

RULER

FELT PENS

TOOTHPICKS

GLUE

1

Cut out a paper rectangle 3 x 1 inches (8 x 3cm). Draw out a grid of small squares with a ruler and pencil.

Kids

2

Fill in alternate squares with black pen, as shown above.

3

Fold the flag in half, then glue it onto a toothpick.

Try making other variations of flag designs. Push the flags into your party sandwiches.

FILLMORE'S TOP TIP:
MAKE SURE YOU MAKE YOUR FRIENDS HEALTHY FOOD SUCH AS THESE TUNA AND CUCUMBER SANDWICHES!

RAMONE

- **VEHICLE:** 1959 CHEVROLET IMPALA LOWRIDER
- **COLOUR:** PURPLE WITH YELLOW AND ORANGE FLAMES
- **PROS:** NEVER GETS BORED WITH THE WAY HE LOOKS
- **PROFILE:**

  Owner of the **HOUSE OF BODY ART**, he's the most artistic and colourful resident of **RADIATOR SPRINGS**. He **LOVES** to paint himself and other cars, too. He is married to **FLO** who runs the **V8 CAFÉ**. His favourite catchphrase is 'LOW AND SLOW'.

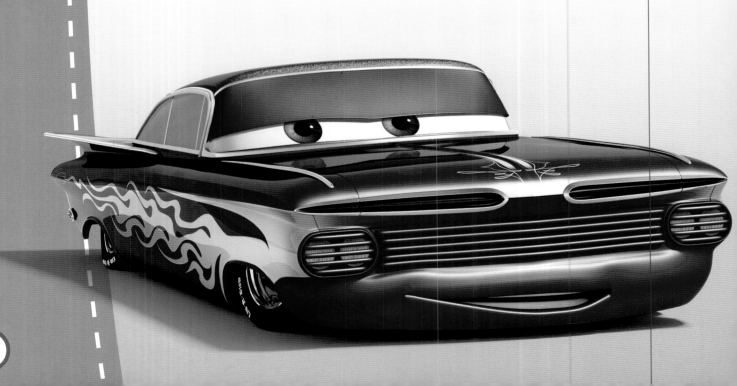

BLUE RAMONE

Ramone was in his House of Body Art painting himself blue, when Lightning and Mater turned up.

Ramone explained that Flo was having a birthday party and that her favourite colour was blue. "Gee whiz!" said Mater in surprise.

That night, the town gathered in Main Street for Flo's birthday party. "Oh, Ramone!" Flo exclaimed when she saw his blue paintwork. As Flo and Ramone cruised down the street, the rest of the cars watched. Then Ramone made an announcement to everybody. "In honour of Flo's birthday, I promise to stay blue for one full week!" he shouted.

The next day, Ramone got up early and started cleaning his shop. After he'd finished, he was tempted to paint himself a new colour – but then he remembered his promise. Ramone stayed blue the next day and the next. He kept asking all the cars in town if they wanted paint jobs, but they didn't. Ramone had to paint something!

Flo could see there was something wrong. She said to Ramone that if he wanted to paint himself a new colour, he should go ahead and do it! Mater agreed and encouraged Ramone to just be himself.

Everyone missed the happy, freshly-painted Ramone. So Ramone happily went to work painting himself every colour he could find!

TURN THE PAGE

GIVE YOUR T-SHIRT A LICK OF PAINT, JUST LIKE RAMONE!

STRIKING T-SHIRT

This t-shirt makes an impact and what's the best thing about it? The fact that you designed it and made it! It's an original just like Ramone!

YOU WILL NEED

A PLAIN T SHIRT

TAPE

CARD – TO GO INSIDE T-SHIRT

PENCIL

SCISSORS

THIN CARD TO MAKE STENCIL

SPONGE PIECES

FABRIC PAINTS – FOLLOW MANUFACTURER'S INSTRUCTIONS

FABRIC PEN FOR OUTLINING IN BLACK

1

Push a piece of card inside the T-shirt. Make sure there are no creases.

2

Draw a big lightning bolt shape onto card. Make sure it will fit the shape of your T-shirt then cut it out so you have a stencil.

Kids
3

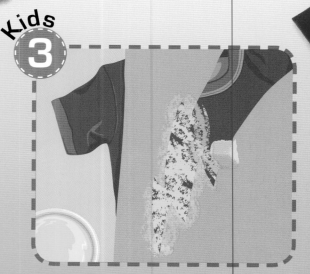

Tape the card stencil over the T-shirt. Dip a sponge into yellow paint, dab it off onto newspaper so the paint isn't too wet, then sponge over the lightning strike.

RAMONE'S TOP TIP:
REMEMBER YOU CAN BE INSPIRED
BY ANYTHING AROUND YOU!
IF YOU LIKE IT, DESIGN IT!

Sponge orange paint onto some bubble wrap and press it down over the top of the lightning shape to make a dotted pattern. Dry and outline in a black fabric pen.

LIGHTNING BOLT KEY CHAIN

This cool looking key chain is very flashy! Make it, paint it, wear it!

1

Mix up 2 cups (200g) of plain flour and 1 cup (200g) of salt in a mixing bowl. Add 1 cup (200ml) of water, and 1 tablespoon oil to make a dough.

YOU WILL NEED

SALT DOUGH RECIPE:	OTHER:
2 CUPS (200G) PLAIN FLOUR	PAPER
1 CUP (200G) OF SALT	PENCIL
1 CUP (200ML) OF WATER	A ROLLING PIN
1 TABLESPOON OF COOKING OIL	A KNIFE
	PENCIL
	A BAKING TRAY
	PAINT
	A KEY CHAIN

2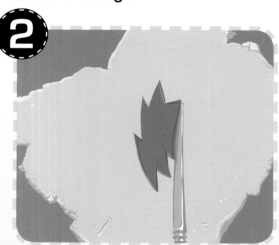

Knead the dough into a ball on a floured work surface. Roll it out to 1½ inch (1cm) thick. Place a card lightning shape onto the rolled dough and cut around it.

3

Make a small hole in the middle using the tip of a pencil. Set hard. It may take a couple of days to dry out thoroughly or you can oven dry in three hours at a very low temperature.

Paint the lightning in yellow and red. Leave to dry before attaching to a key chain.

LIGHTNING'S TOP TIP: HANG THIS KEY CHAIN FROM YOUR FAVOURITE RUCKSACK, OR EVEN FROM YOUR PENCIL CASE!

COIN KEEPER

Sally gave up her super rich lifestyle to live in Radiator Springs but she still needs somewhere to keep her coins safe!

You will need

EMPTY CARDBOARD CONTAINER WITH LID

RULER AND PENCIL

SEVERAL 8½ X 11 INCH (21.5 X 28CM) SHEETS OF COLOURED PAPER

WHITE GLUE AND BRUSH

CRAFT KNIFE OR BOX CUTTER

1

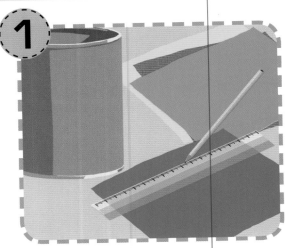

Measure the height of the container and cut the paper to the same height. Draw narrow and wide lines down one sheet.

2

Put the ruled sheet with the lines drawn on it on top of the others and cut along the lines to make long strips.

Kids 3

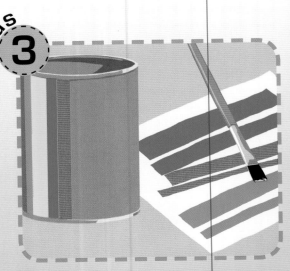

Paint the strips with glue and stick them to the can, making sure they overlap and smoothing them down carefully.

4

After the glue has dried, cut a slot measuring about 2 x ¼ inches (5 x 1cm).

SALLY'S TOP TIP:
IF YOU DON'T LIKE THE IDEA OF MULTI-COLOURS ON YOUR COIN KEEPER TRY JUST A COUPLE OR EVEN ONE!

SHERIFF'S BADGE

Make some salt dough, then model yourself a lawman's badge. Flash it if you dare and run those bad guys out of town!

YOU WILL NEED

SALT DOUGH RECIPE:

2 CUPS (200G) PLAIN FLOUR

1 CUP (200G) OF SALT

1 CUP (200ML) OF WATER

1 TABLESPOON OF COOKING OIL

½ RECIPE SALT DOUGH

STAR-SHAPED COOKIE CUTTER

COOKIE SHEET, GREASED

SILVER PAINT AND BRUSH

SAFETY PIN

ALL-PURPOSE GLUE

1

Mix up 2 cups (200g) of plain flour and 1 cup (200g) of salt in a mixing bowl. Add 1 cup (200ml) of water, and 1 tablespoon oil to make a dough.

2

Roll out the dough to about ¼ inch (0.5cm) thick. Cut out some star shapes with the cookie cutter and put them onto a greased cookie sheet.

3

Make as many tiny balls as your star has points. Wet the corners of the stars and stick a ball on each corner. Let dry for up to three days. Paint the star silver and let dry. Glue a safety pin to the back to the star.

SHERIFF'S GAME IDEA: GET THREE OR MORE FRIENDS TOGETHER. ONE PLAYER IS THE SHERIFF AND WEARS THE BADGE. THE OTHER PLAYERS HIDE — THEY ARE CARS ON THE RUN FROM SHERIFF! ONCE FOUND, A PLAYER BECOMES A SHERIFF, WEARS THE BADGE AND HELPS LOOK FOR ALL THE OTHERS!

BOOK OF COOL STUFF

The King collects cool mementos from his racing wins in a scrapbook. Make your own book of cool stuff whether it's racing themed or just stuff you really like!

YOU WILL NEED

- A SCRAPBOOK
- CARD - CUT FROM CARDBOARD BOX OR CEREAL PACKET IS FINE
- MASKING TAPE
- TORN PAPER STRIPS
- CORRUGATED CARD
- OLD NEWSPAPERS OR MAGAZINES
- PAINTS
- STENCIL LETTERS
- SPONGE
- GLUE
- SCISSORS

Kids 1

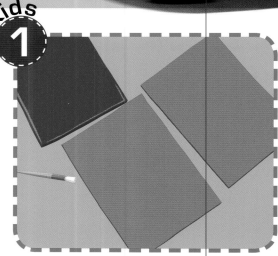

Cut two pieces of card the same size as your scrapbook. Cover them in (blue) paint and leave to dry.

2

Glue one piece of card to the front of the scrapbook and one piece to the back. Tape down the spine.

Kids 3

Sponge paint onto the corrugated card. Use this to print a pattern onto the paper strips. Sponge paint through the stencil lettering onto strips. Leave to dry.

Glue the printed strips of paper onto the front of your scrapbook. Add some torn pieces of newspaper or old magazines to finish off your cool design.

THE KING'S TOP TIP:
USE A CAMERA OR CAMERA PHONE TO TAKE PICTURES OF ANYTHING COOL YOU SPOT WHILE YOU ARE OUT AND ABOUT TO BE IN YOUR BOOK!

COOL STUFF

BIGGEST FAN POSTER

Are you Lightning's number one fan like Mia and Tia? To show your appreciation make this fan poster and put it up on your bedroom wall.

YOU WILL NEED

A BIG PIECE OF CARD FOR THE BANNER 20 X 28 INCHES (50CM X 70CM)

CARD – FOR THE HANDLES

FOIL

THIN CARD FOR THE LETTERS

SCISSORS

PENCIL

RULER

GLUE AND TAPE

1

Draw a circle around a plate onto thick card then cut it out. Cut the circle into two handle shapes for the banner. Brush with glue, then cover with foil.

2

LIGHTNING McQUEEN IS MY CHAMP!

25

Draw out the first letter inside the rectangle. Cut it out.

3

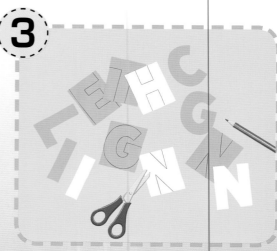

Do the same for the other letters. If you draw them all inside the rectangle they will be the same size.

4

Glue the letters onto the cardboard to spell out your message. Put it up on your wall for everyone to see!

MIA AND TIA'S TOP TIP: MAKE SURE YOU USE BRIGHT PAPER FOR YOUR POSTER. YOU WANT IT TO STAND OUT ON YOUR WALL!

FLAMING HOT SHOES

These totally, TOTALLY cool shoes have the hottest design on them...quite literally!

1

Use the paint to draw and colour pictures on your sneakers. Here are scary skulls. Boo! Let dry.

YOU WILL NEED

PAIR OF CLEAN SNEAKERS OR CANVAS SHOES

FABRIC PAINTS

FABRIC PENS

Kids
2

Next, add some more detail in a different coloured paint, like these flames. Let dry.

Kids
3

Once you've finished your design on both shoes, leave them to dry thoroughly.

4

Sometimes the paint shrinks a little as it dries and flakes off. Touch up with some fresh paint or fabric pens!

5

Now you're ready to wear your totally unique footwear.

RAMONE'S TOP TIP:
MAKE SURE YOU REALLY PLAN YOUR DESIGN FIRST SO YOU ARE TOTALLY HAPPY WITH THE FINISH!

SARGE

- **VEHICLE:** 1942 WWII WILLY'S ARMY JEEP

- **COLOUR:** KHAKI GREEN

- **PROS:** A BORN FIGHTER WITH GRIT AND DETERMINATION

- **PROFILE:**

  Has a surplus store named 'SARGE'S SURPLUS HUT', nextdoor to FILLMORE, and is part of LIGHTNING'S pit crew. Sarge also runs his BOOT CAMP where he trains 4X4S in rugged and dirt terrain including T.J. Hummer, Murphy, Frank "Pinky" Pinkerton and Charlie Cargo.

SARGE'S BOOT CAMP

Sarge had decided to start a training camp for all 4x4s arriving at Radiator Springs. Sarge shouted out orders as Guido and Luigi raced down Main Street. Sheriff turned on his head lights and siren, and yelled at them to slow down.

Just then a new 4x4 rolled into town. "Hi, I'm T.J." said the 4x4.

Sarge yelled out to the newcomer as he welcomed T.J. to Radiator Springs and his boot camp! Sarge led the group out of town to a rocky dirt road. T.J. was already complaining of dirt getting into his grille and his spark plugs shaking loose. Sarge ordered everyone to go down a steep slope and across a big, muddy puddle. T.J. gasped and was afraid he was going to flip over. Sarge called out. "Show a bit of courage, soldier!" Guido and Luigi encouraged T.J. too. "Come on!" Luigi called to T.J. "You're a 4x4! This should be no problem!" Although T.J. was dirty, his paintwork scratched and he was tired, he soon laughed as he reached the bottom of the slope.

T.J. thanked Guido and Luigi for their encouragement. As they looked up at the steep hill now in front of them, T.J. called to his friends to hop onto his roof rack. Together the cars raced up the hill and back to town – excited about the next day of Sarge's boot camp!

TURN THE PAGE

MAKE A STORE FOR YOUR OFF-ROAD KIT!

CHAMPION STORAGE

Sarge know it's important to keep everything in order. That's why you need a cool box to keep your party stuff safe and organized before the main event!

Kids 1

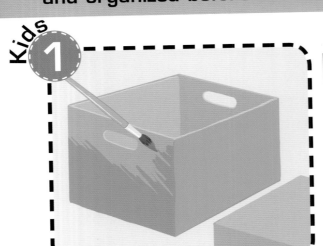

Paint the box and the lid in your favourite colour. Leave to dry, then paint a second coat.

YOU WILL NEED

LARGE CARDBOARD BOX WITH LID

LARGE AND SMALL PAINTBRUSHES

ACRYLIC PAINTS

PENCIL

PAPER

SCISSORS

WHITE GLUE AND BRUSH

Kids 2

Draw different pieces of sport equipment (or whatever designs you wish) onto the white paper. Cut them out.

Kids 3

Use paints to colour in the sporting shapes.

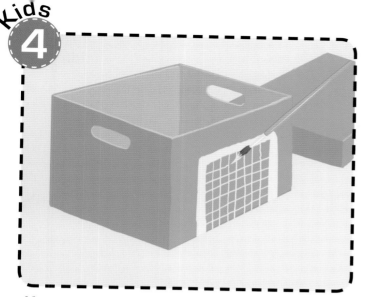

If you wish, paint a large white football net, or some other design onto the front of the box.

Arrange all the sports shapes around the box and glue them on.

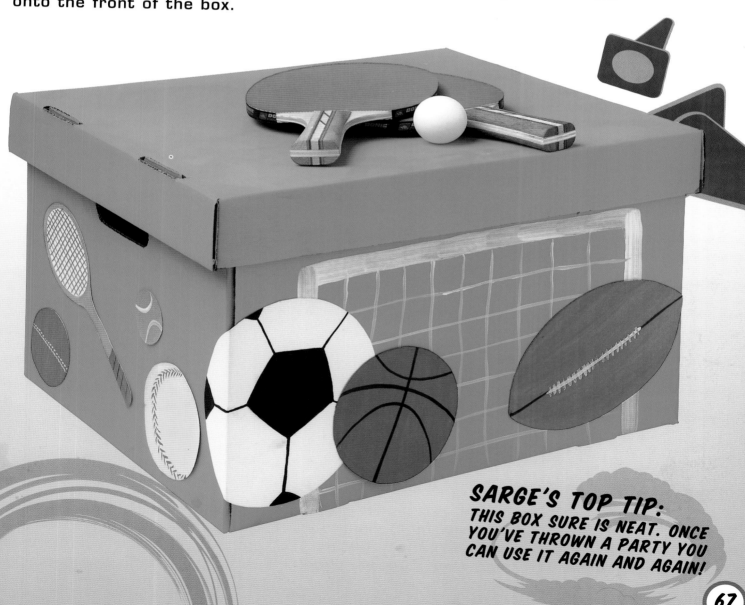

SARGE'S TOP TIP:
THIS BOX SURE IS NEAT. ONCE YOU'VE THROWN A PARTY YOU CAN USE IT AGAIN AND AGAIN!

PODIUM BOOKENDS

Chick Hicks knows how to show off on the racetrack, now you can show off your books and cool stuff with these bookends!

YOU WILL NEED

- 3 SMALL BOXES
- TAPE (PREFERABLY MASKING TAPE)
- GLUE AND SCISSORS
- PEBBLES / LARGE STONES
- PAINT
- COLOURED CARD

1

Place the three boxes for your podium together to check the sizes for positions 1, 2 and 3 on the podium. Cut them down if you need to, leaving flaps.

Kids 2

Put a pebble inside each box then tape the flaps securely so the pebbles won't fall out. If the flaps aren't big enough, tape a piece of card to cover the end.

Kids 3

Paint the boxes and leave them to dry. Glue the three boxes together. Position the largest box in the middle and the two smaller ones on either side.

CHICK HICK'S TOP TIP: YOU CAN DISPLAY YOUR FAVOURITE TOYS ON THE PODIUMS!

④ Cut out numbers 1, 2 and 3 from the yellow card, then stick them onto the boxes. Or you could cut a circle from card and draw the numbers in felt pen.

SECRET BOOK BOX

Sheriff has to keep a lot of case facts secret and safe. Keep your secrets inside this cool box!

YOU WILL NEED

EMPTY CEREAL BOX

8½ X 11 INCHES (21.5 X 28CM) OF WHITE CARDBOARD

SCISSORS

PENCIL AND RULER

WHITE GLUE AND BRUSH

RED RIBBON

BLACK PAINT

RED AND BLACK CARD

1

Cut the front of the empty box around three sides. Leave the left side uncut so it makes a flap.

Kids
2

Using the pencil and ruler, draw straight lines on the white cardboard. Using the box as a guide, cut out three pieces of cardboard to fit around the sides of the box. Glue them in place.

3

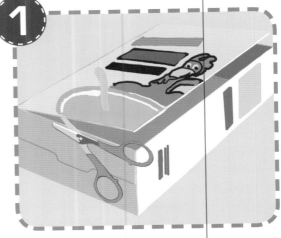

Cut the ribbon in half and glue one piece to the back of the box and the other to the front flap, halfway down.

4

Paint the box on the front and spine in black paint. Leave to dry. Paint the reverse of the box black. Leave to dry.

5

Cut out a rectangle of red card to cover the spine. Cut out a black rectangle and glue to the spine. Cut out a red rectangle and slightly smaller black rectangle from the card for the front of the box. Glue the red card to the front. Dry. Then glue the black on top of the red card. Dry.

SHERIFF'S TOP TIP:
WANT TO ADD A BOLT OF COLOUR? ADD COOL DETAILS TO YOUR BOX LIKE THIS FLASH OF LIGHTNING!

DVD HOLDER

Create this dynamically different DVD holder inspired by the one and only electrifying D.J..

YOU WILL NEED

A CARDBOARD BOX - CHOOSE A BOX SLIGHTLY BIGGER THAN THE DEPTH OF A DVD.

GLUE

CARD - A CEREAL BOX IS A GOOD THICKNESS

PAINT

SCISSORS

BRUSH

FOIL

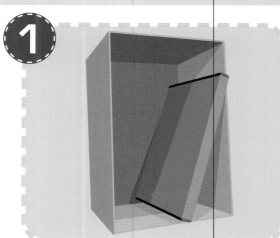

1 Cut a cardboard box to the right size for a DVD to fit inside, leaving a small gap at the top.

Kids
2

Paint the box – bright blue on the outside, dark blue inside. Dry.

3

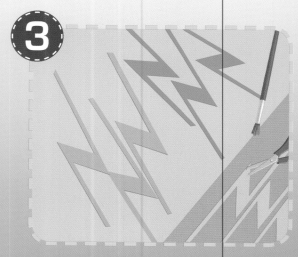

Cut some long Z-shaped pieces from card. Paint them in 2 different greens. Dry.

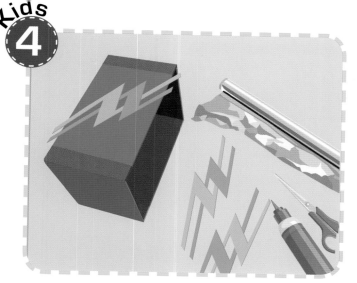

Stick foil strips around the edges of the box. Stick the green Z's to the box. Now you're all set to put your most favourite DVD's inside!

D.J.'S TOP TIP:
YOU COULD MAKE ANOTHER BOX TO STORE YOUR BEST GAMES TOO! ONE FOR EACH.

CAR-RAZY CHEQUERED POSTER

Want to make your room a racing haven? Then make this chequered wall frieze and place on your walls!

1

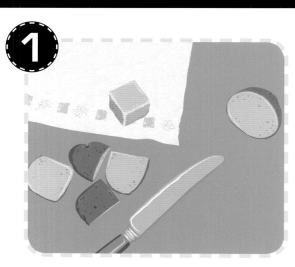

Cut a potato in half. Cut the end of one half into a square. Make the square about 1 x 1 inches (3 x 3cm).

YOU WILL NEED

LONG 30 INCHES (70CM) STRIPS OF PAPER - RED AND WHITE

A POTATO

A KNIFE

PAINT

RULER

PENCIL

2

Measure out a long strip of white paper, make it four times wider than the potato square. Measure out two strips of red paper, make them the same width as the potato square.

Kids 3

Stick the red strips onto either side of the white strip.

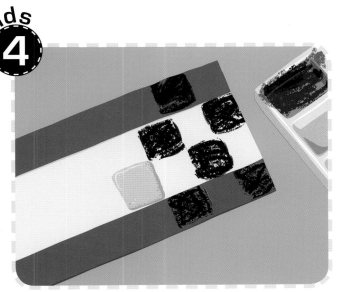

Dip the potato into black paint and print squares onto the strips. Dry. Then position and place on your wall!

LIGHTNING'S TOP TIP: RACING ISN'T JUST BLACK AND WHITE. YOU COULD TRY DIFFERENT CONTRASTING COLOURS FOR YOUR FLAG.

BRIGHT BEAN BAGS

These brightly coloured bean bags are almost as blinding as Snot Rod's body work.

Kids

1

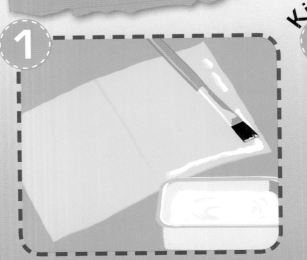

2

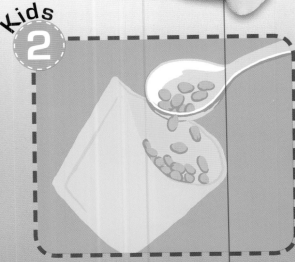

Take each felt rectangle and spread glue along one of the longer edges and along one of the shorter edges. Fold it in half and let the glue dry.

Using a spoon fill the felt bag about two-thirds full with the dried beans or lentils. Turn the bag so the longest glued edge is facing you.

SNOT ROD'S TOP TIP: IF YOU DON'T KNOW HOW TO JUGGLE START BY PLAYING A SIMPLE THROW AND CATCH GAME WITH A FRIEND!

Kids

3

4

Brush glue inside the top of the bag and press the edges together to make the pyramid shape. Let dry.

Using the needle and thread, sew a pom-pom onto each of the four corners of the juggling bags.

DOOR HANGER

Wingo's bodyart is loud and proud and so is this door hanger! Hang this from your bedroom door with pride!

YOU WILL NEED

- RED CARD
- GLUE AND SAFETY SCISSORS
- STRAWS
- SPONGE
- PAINT
- YELLOW PAPER
- PRE-CUT FOAM LETTERS

Kids 1

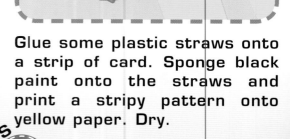

Glue some plastic straws onto a strip of card. Sponge black paint onto the straws and print a stripy pattern onto yellow paper. Dry.

2

Arrange the foam letters to spell out your message. Cut a piece of (red) card big enough for the message to fit on, then glue down the letters leaving a space at the top.

Kids 3

Cut out a circle of black card. Us the straws to print a tyre patter around the edge of the circle. Di them in paint and print. Leave t dry.

4 Glue strips cut from the yellow stripy paper around the edge. Glue the tyre at the top. Cut a hole into the middle so it can be hung onto a door handle.

WINGO'S TOP TIP: MAKE SURE A GROWN UP HELPS YOU WITH THE LETTERS. OR YOU COULD JUST WRITE DIRECTLY ONTO YOUR HANGER.

PIT STOP CREW

DO NOT ENTER

AL OFT BLIMP

○ **VEHICLE: AN AIRSHIP**

○ **COLOUR: BLUE, WHITE AND YELLOW**

○ **PROS: HAS A BIRDS EYE VIEW OF RADIATOR SPRINGS**

○ **PROFILE:**

The *LIGHTYEAR BLIMP* is an airship. He flies above the racetrack and records overhead footage of the race with his video camera. His name, *AL OFT*, is a reference to "*ALOFT*" meaning '*IN FLIGHT*'.

AL'S SKY HIGH ADVENTURE

Al Oft, the Lightyear Blimp, would hover above the big stadium during races. Fans cheered whenever they saw Al flying above, but he was lonely up in the sky all by himself. After the race season, Al decided to fly over the countryside. One day, as he was flying low, he spotted Lightning!

Lightning called out to Al and welcomed him to Radiator Springs. Mater explained that a stray tractor had busted loose, and they couldn't find it. They asked Al to help them find the tractor. Sure enough, from high in the sky, Al soon found the lost tractor between some big rocks. Al was able to find a path for Lightning and Mater to drive through and within minutes, they were guiding the tractor home.

To celebrate, Lightning invited Al to the neon cruise they were holding that evening. "But I can't cruise," said Al sadly. "Sure you can!" said Lightning. "Just turn on your neon and fly low."

As the cars in Radiator Springs looked up at Al, Lightning introduced him. Al smiled. He was having the most fun he'd ever had. And with all his new friends, he knew he'd never be lonely again.

TURN THE PAGE

MAKE SOME HIGH-FLYING PLANES WITH BLIMP!

RACING PLANES

Blimp always has a birds eye view of every race. How about you take the race to him with these aerial bound racers!?

Kids 1

Fold the sheet of paper in half. Turn down the corners at one end so that the folded-down edges line up along your fold.

YOU WILL NEED

SQUARE SHEET OF COLOURED PAPER

STAPLER AND STAPLES

ROUND STICKERS OR PAINT FOR DECORATION

Kids 2

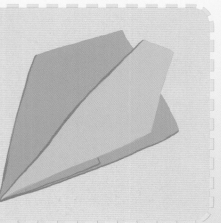

To make the wings, fold the top down again, lining it up along the bottom of the shape. Repeat on the other side.

Kids 3

Fold the top flaps down again, lining them up along the bottom of the airplane.

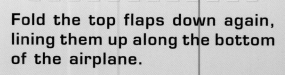

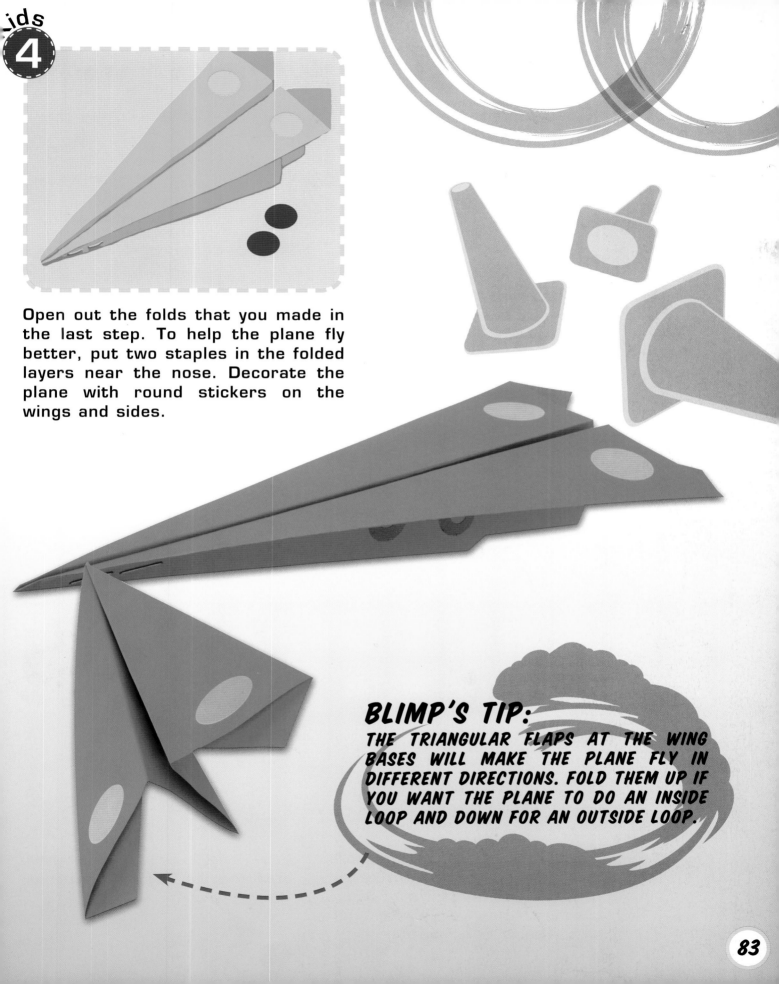

Open out the folds that you made in the last step. To help the plane fly better, put two staples in the folded layers near the nose. Decorate the plane with round stickers on the wings and sides.

BLIMP'S TIP:
THE TRIANGULAR FLAPS AT THE WING BASES WILL MAKE THE PLANE FLY IN DIFFERENT DIRECTIONS. FOLD THEM UP IF YOU WANT THE PLANE TO DO AN INSIDE LOOP AND DOWN FOR AN OUTSIDE LOOP.

RACE CREW BADGES

Chick Hick's race crew all play an important role on race day. And it's just as important to know who everyone is! That's why you have badges!

YOU WILL NEED

CARD OR CRAFT FOAM

A PENCIL

PRINTED MESSAGES

GLUE AND TAPE

SAFETY PINS

PAINT

CORRUGATED CARD

1

Print out some messages for your badges. Cut them out. Either use a printer or write out your messages on paper.

Kids
2

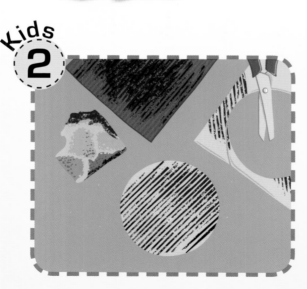

Print stripes using corrugated card to make a patterned background. Draw and cut out other shapes from card, such as tools or lightning bolts.

3

Glue the printed messages onto the cut out card shapes.

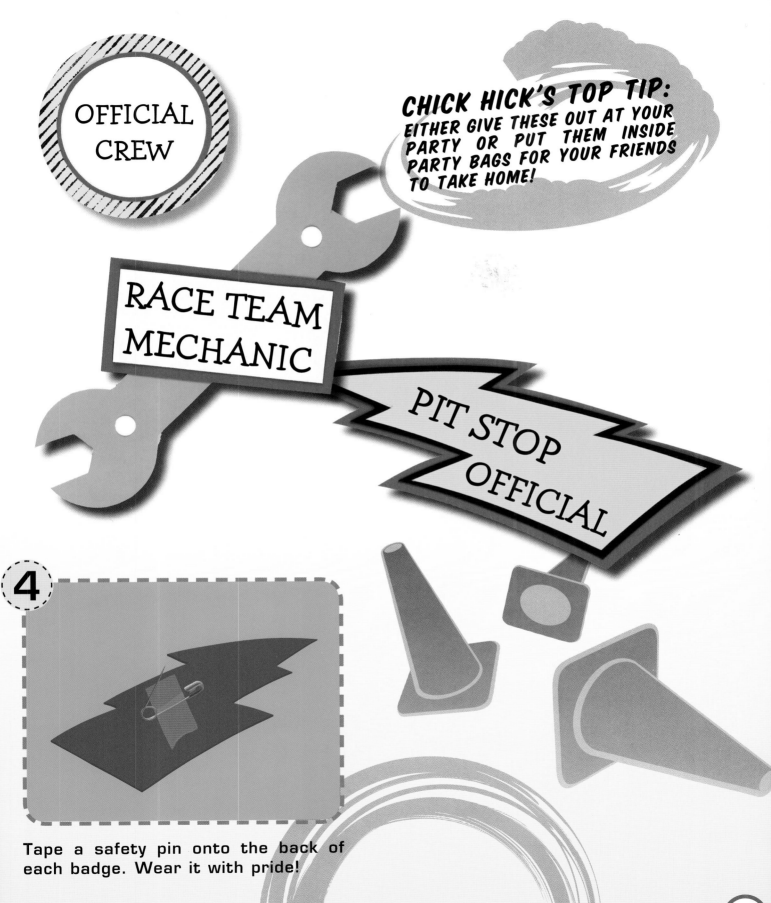

OFFICIAL CREW

CHICK HICK'S TOP TIP: EITHER GIVE THESE OUT AT YOUR PARTY OR PUT THEM INSIDE PARTY BAGS FOR YOUR FRIENDS TO TAKE HOME!

RACE TEAM MECHANIC

PIT STOP OFFICIAL

4 Tape a safety pin onto the back of each badge. Wear it with pride!

RACE BOATS

For more party game fun, hit the water with these sailboats and race your boat across the finish line.

Kids 1

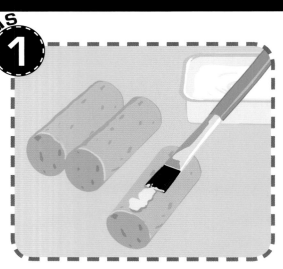

Glue the corks together, side by side. Let dry.

YOU WILL NEED

FOR EACH BOAT:

3 CORKS

WHITE GLUE AND BRUSH

2 LARGE CRAFT STICKS

TOOTHPICK

SCRAPS OF COLOURED PAPER

Kids 2

Glue the two sticks to the top of the corks as shown. Let dry.

3

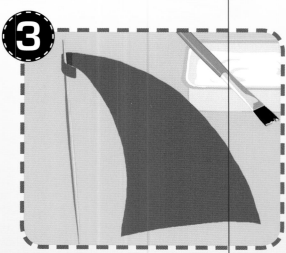

Cut a triangular sail from some coloured paper. Apply a little glue to the tip of the sail and wrap it around the top of the toothpick mast. Let dry.

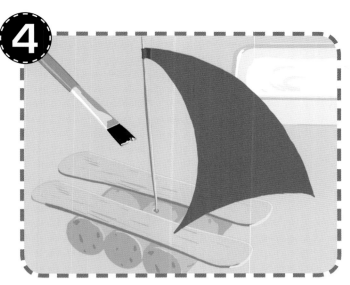

4 Make a hole in the centre of the middle cork between the sticks. Push the toothpick mast into the hole. Bend the sail so it sits on the top of the boat.

5 Cut a tiny triangle in yellow paper and glue to the top of the toothpick mast to make a flag.

LIGHTNING'S TOP TIP: ADD THESE LIGHTNING FLASHES TO MAKE YOUR SAILBOATS LOOK EXTRA COOL.

TRUCKER HAT

Mack is always wearing his stylish trucker hat where ever he goes. To get noticed at your party try making your own. Lookin' good!

Kids 1

Outline the eye area and lightning bolts in pencil, then fill them in with a brush using white and yellow paint. Allow to dry. Dip a cork into some blue paint. Carefully press the cork onto the white area to print blue circles for the eyes. Allow to dry.

2

Add black middles to the eyes with a marker and outline the eye area and lightning bolt in black.

YOU WILL NEED

A PLAIN CAP	BRUSH
AN OLD TOWEL OR T-SHIRT TO COVER YOURSELF	PERMANENT MARKER/FABRIC PEN
PENCIL	A CORK
PAINTS – FABRIC PAINT IS PREFERABLE	COTTON SWAB

Kids 3

Add orange dots to the lightning bolt with a cotton swab and then add white paint highlights to the pupils.

88

PENCIL POT

Keep all your brightest colouring pencils or crayons in this pot. Can your pencils compete with Snot Rod's fiery body art?

YOU WILL NEED

EMPTY CARDBOARD TUBE

ABOUT 30 ICE-CREAM STICKS OF THE SAME SIZE

SMALL SET SQUARE (TRIANGLE)

WHITE GLUE AND BRUSH

SNOT ROD'S TOP TIP: ADD SOME COLOUR DECORATE WITH PAINTS OR STICKERS!

Kids

1

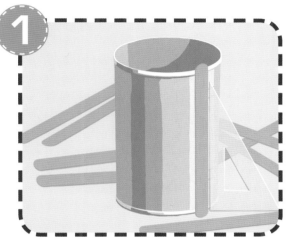

Wash the sticks and tube. When dry, line up the set square against the tube and glue the stick in place, aligning it with the set square. Let dry.

2

Glue the sticks around the tube, until it's completely covered. Make sure the sticks align snugly.

TYRE TRACK FRAME

Mack has the biggest tyres as he is one big truck! Create this tyre themed frame to show off your favourite pictures!

YOU WILL NEED

THICK CARD
(CARDBOARD BOX)

MASKING TAPE

TOY CAR OR TRUCK

PAINTS

SMALL SPONGE

SCISSORS

1

Cut 2 'L' shapes from card that is about 8 x 1½ inches (20 x 4cm) in size.

2

Tape the two pieces together to make a frame then paint it black. Leave to dry.

3

Sponge paint onto the wheels of a toy car or truck then roll it around the frame slowly pressing down so it leaves a clear track mark.

4

Wipe the wheels clean then repeat using a different colour. Tape a photo inside when the paint has dried.

MACK'S TOP TIP:
YOU CAN PUT ANYTHING IN YOUR FRAME. YOUR BEST FRIEND, YOUR FAVOURITE BAND OR EVEN YOUR FAVOURITE TRUCK!

VEGGIE VEHICLES

Get creative with a cucumber or carrot in this car-razy make from Fillmore!

YOU WILL NEED

A SELECTION OF FRUIT AND VEGETABLES, SOME PRE-SLICED

WOODEN SKEWERS

COCKTAILS STICKS

ELASTIC BANDS

1

Push two wooden skewers through a large vegetable like a courgette, aubergine, cucumber or melon.

Kids
2

Push four matching pieces of fruit onto the each ends of the skewers, such as apples, small oranges, or slices of courgette.

3

Stretch elastic bands between axels to stop the 'wheels' rolling off.

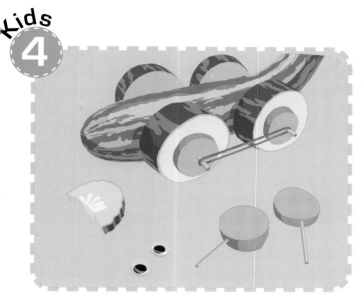

Add other slices of fruit or vegetables to make the eyes and other parts of your vehicle.

FILLMORE'S GAME TIP: LET'S SEE WHO CAN MAKE THE BEST VEHICLE FROM THEIR VEGGIES IN ONLY FIVE MINUTES! PLAY THIS TIMED GAME FOR EXTRA FUN!

PISTON CUP TROPHY

The King has held a few trophies in his time. If you're a champ in the making you'll need your very own trophy!

YOU WILL NEED

CARD FROM A CARDBOARD BOX	PENCIL
	RULER
PAPER – TO MAKE A TEMPLATE	GLUE
	PAINT – GOLD,
SCISSORS	BLACK

1

Fold some paper 8 x 14 inches (21 x 36cm) in half. See the picture above. Draw the shape onto the paper and then cut out the base and sides, to form the cup shape. Open the paper, you now have a symmetrical cup shape to draw around onto cardboard.

2

Draw one of the handle shapes and the cup base onto paper. Cut them out. Trace around your paper templates onto cardboard. You will need two handle shapes (facing opposite ways).

3

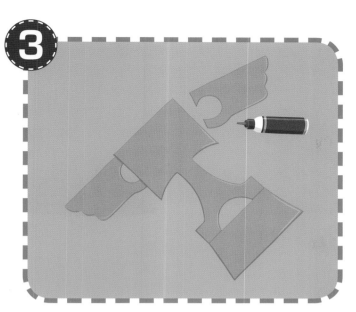

Kids 4

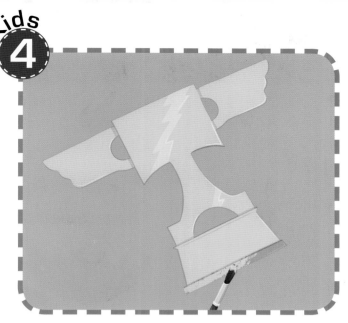

Glue the cut out card shapes together, as shown above. If there are any rough edges cover these with strips of masking tape.

Paint the cup in gold. Add two coats if necessary. Then add thin lines of black paint across the top of the cup, and paint the base black, leaving a gold area for the name plate.

THE KING'S GAME TIP:
THIS IS A FUN ADDITION TO A PARTY. ONCE YOU HAVE PLAYED PARTY GAMES OR HELD A RACE THE WINNERS CAN POSE WITH THIS TROPHY!

95

PICK-UP STICKS

To win this game you'll need a racing champ's nerves of steel. Be careful though, one false move and you'll be out!

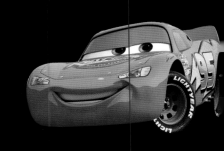

1

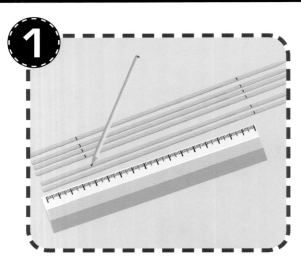

Line up six sticks in a row. Use a pencil and ruler to mark each stick 1½ inches (4cm) from each end.

Kids 2

Paint the ends of the six sticks red up to the marks you made. Make orange, green, and blue sets in the same way. Paint the last stick purple all over.

YOU WILL NEED

25 WOODEN STICKS

ACRYLIC PAINTS: RED, ORANGE, GREEN, BLUE, PURPLE

THIN PAINTBRUSH

RULER AND PENCIL

LIGHTNING'S GAME TIPS:

DROP ALL THE STICKS EXCEPT THE PURPLE ONE IN A RANDOM HEAP. EACH PLAYER TAKES A TURN TO TRY TO REMOVE STICKS FROM THE PILE, ONE BY ONE, USING THE PURPLE STICK TO HELP. YOU MUST ONLY TOUCH THE STICK YOU ARE AIMING FOR, OTHERWISE YOUR TURN IS OVER!